Going Viral
Communication Techniques for Social Media Success

Table of Contents

Chapter 1. Introduction

Welcome to your guide to digitizing your influence with our special report, "Going Viral: Communication Techniques for Social Media Success!" Have you ever seen content that's travelled around the globe, acquiring millions of likes, shares, and comments at blazing speed, and wondered, "How did they do it?" From engaging tweets to traffic-stopping Instagram posts, this report is bursting with industry secrets, proven strategies, and expert tips to elevate your brand to the pinnacle of digital recognition. Prepare to unlock the power of social media and earn your moment in the online spotlight, all whilst having the time of your life! You're just a click away from transforming your online presence! Let's make your message matter, let's make it viral!

Chapter 2. Understanding the DNA of Viral Content

Like any living organism, every piece of content that goes viral has its own unique DNA, a genetic blueprint of sorts that determines two things: its potential to spread and the speed at which it will do so. Understanding this DNA is not only key to shape your own successful viral campaign, but it's also a fascinating exploration of human psychology and social behavior.

Let's dissect the DNA of viral content, pinpoint its qualities and components, and shed light on how to infuse these into your own content to maximize its virality potential.

2.1. The Emotional Connective Tissue

Powerful emotions are the engine driving the rapid spread of viral content. Content that resonates with viewers on an emotional level is more likely to be shared, and the stronger the emotional reaction, the faster the content spreads. This emotional resonance can be achieved through various ways, be it startling revelations, heartfelt stories, hilarious jokes, or awe-inspiring visuals.

Does this mean your content should always aim to provide emotional rollercoasters? Not necessarily. The key aspect here is relatability. Whether positive or negative, the emotion your content ignites needs to resonate with your audience's experiences, values, or desires.

2.2. The Power of Social Currency

Each share, like, or comment on social media is a reflection of our identities. We share content that makes us seem intelligent, benevolent, funny, or insightful to our social circles. As a result, content that provides social currency – makes people look good in the eyes of others – tends to go viral. To put it simply, it's about creating something share-worthy that enhances the sharer's image, credibility or status.

2.3. The Practicality Principle

Practical, valuable content has a greater chance of going viral. This is because it fulfills a basic human instinct: the desire to help others. By providing content that can potentially benefit others, you tap into this instinct, enhancing your content's shareability factor. This could be a life hack, advice column, a tutorial video, or an informative infographic.

2.4. The Storytelling Structure

Humans have been trading stories since the dawn of civilization. They are an integral part of how we understand and navigate the world. This universal love for stories, particularly those with compelling narratives or characters, can be harnessed to enhance your content's virality.

Storytelling doesn't imply building fictional narratives. Take for example, a brand narrating its journey, or a product's impact on customers, or even customer success stories, all contribute to the larger narrative of the brand.

2.5. Influencer Outreach: The Catalyst

Imagine an influencer with a substantial following sharing your content. This acts like a spark that can set off a viral wildfire. Reaching out to influencers who resonate with your brand can accelerate the viral process. However, the outreach needs to be genuine and strategic, with influencers who genuinely appreciate your content.

2.6. The Pull of Pop Culture

Viral content often taps into current events or trending pop culture themes. Piggybacking on these trends can significantly enhance the virality of your content by providing familiar hooks that audiences can instantly relate to. However, it's crucial to stay authentic to your brand voice and only utilize trends that align with your brand's image.

2.7. The Essential Role of Timing

Just as a surfer waits for the perfect wave, the release timing of your content can significantly impact its ability to go viral. Analyzing your audience's online behavior patterns and the bigger social media landscape can help you determine the perfect time to launch your viral content bid.

2.8. The Surprise Element

The element of surprise can heavily contribute to your content's virality. Novelty captures attention, curiosity prompts engagement, and surprise sparks sharing. Whether surprising your audience with an unexpected twist, innovative idea, or a shocking revelation, your content's success often hinges on its power to intrigue and astonish.

It's important to remember that while these elements can improve the virality of your content, nothing guarantees a viral success. There's always an element of uncertainty and unpredictability. However, utilizing these will significantly increase the odds of your content being shared far and wide, creating the ripple effect necessary for viral success. Delve deeper, experiment tirelessly, and soon, you might just find your content making headlines in the digital world.

Chapter 3. The Power of Storytelling on Social Media

Approximately, 5 A4 pages of text is around 2750 words. Please find the chapter's comprehensive draft below:

Understanding the human brain is essential to master storytelling. We are hardwired for stories. Since ancient times, individuals have used tales to impart wisdom, cultural traditions, and historical events from one generation to the next. Today, our brains still respond to content by searching for the narrative that promises a captivating experience. Stories stimulate emotions, and those emotions create memories and drive actions.

3.1. Tapping Into the Emotional Reservoir

Stories stir our emotions. When you share a narrative, whether it involves your personal experience, client testimonials, or a case study, you tap into a reservoir of emotions: happiness, sadness, surprise, awe, etc. Activating this emotional journey creates an emotional connection between your audience and your brand, making your message more memorable.

It's essential to remember that emotion drives sharing. People want to share content that moves them. When a story tugs at the heartstrings or kindles jubilant feelings, people are more likely to pass it on to others. Social media becomes the perfect platform for this due to its ease of sharing and vast networks.

3.2. The Hero's Journey Simplified

Your social media story should be modeled on a 'Hero's Journey.' This classic narrative arc, coined by scholar Joseph Campbell, suggests that every human story — from ancient myths to modern movies — falls into a simple structure: Departure, Initiation, and Return.

In Departure, the hero is presented with a challenge they can either accept or reject. In Initiation, the hero takes up the challenge, faces the obstacle, and usually experiences profound transformation. Finally, during the Return phase, the hero brings their newly gained wisdom back to their original world.

3.3. Making Your Audience The Hero

The key to successful storytelling on social media is making your audience into the heroes of your story. Make your product or service the tool they use to conquer their challenge, embodying the transformative power of the Initiation stage. You become the mentor, guiding them through overcoming their own trials.

The crucial part is that your audience must relate to the hero on some level. Whether their challenge is skincare, fitness, personal finance, or home improvement, your product or service should become the game-changer that they've been missing.

3.4. Structuring Your Story for Social Media

The structure you choose for your story can highly impact its performance on social media. Choose a format that is convenient for your audience. Short videos, image-based stories, or text-based posts, each has its own potential. Your choice should align with your audience's consumption habits and the platform you are using.

Focus on a singular message for each story. Don't dilute your central idea with multiple points; keep it lucid and direct. Keep your audience engaged with surprises, humorous content, or little emotional stirs.

3.5. Authentic Narratives Rule

Honesty and authenticity resonate with today's audience. Authentic stories increase brand trust and loyalty. Social media users crave real-world stories, and they gravitate towards brands that offer genuine narratives. Show the challenges you've faced, the adversities you've overcome, and the transformations you've achieved. This will make your brand more relatable and trustworthy.

3.6. Dine Out on Data

Use data to refine your social media storytelling strategy. Which posts are getting more responses? What are the demographics of individuals engaging with your posts? What times of the day show most activity? Use this collected data to optimize your storytelling strategy. A perfect blend of creativity and data analysis can help your brand's story spread wider and deeper into your target demographics.

3.7. Conclusion

Storytelling is an incredibly potent tool in the digital sphere. The stories that we share on social media give us the opportunity to connect on a deeper level, help us build relationships and create an active community around our brand. If done right, storytelling can be the core of your social media strategy taking your brand from the shadows into the viral spotlight. It's time to tell your story, make it compelling; make it viral!

Chapter 4. Building a Magnetic Social Media Presence

Before diving into specific strategies for crafting your magnetic social media presence, understanding the unique traits that each social media platform has to offer is essential. Accurate knowledge will enable you to tailor your content to maximize its potential and acquire the greatest level of engagement.

4.1. Understanding Different Social Media Platforms

Different social media platforms have different strengths, and your content creation strategy should reflect these variations. Let's explore some of the most popular platforms and what they're best for.

Twitter is small but mighty; the platform is most effective for real-time communication. This includes news updates, live reporting, public relations, brand announcements, and for a quick exchange of thoughts.

On the other hand, **Instagram** is a visually-oriented channel that thrives on stunning imagery, short video clips, behind-the-scenes shots, and aesthetics. This platform allows businesses to showcase their products in action or display services attractively.

LinkedIn is a professional networking site that serves as a platform for thought leadership, industry updates, professional insights, and business networking. Content such as informative articles, company news, and professional achievements performs best here.

Facebook, the giant of social media, is a melting pot of all content types. You can share blogs, updates, photos, videos, join groups, and even host live chats. Facebook suits both B2C and B2B businesses and allows you to connect more informally with your audience.

4.2. Crafting Your Social Media Strategy

A solid social media strategy is vital for ensuring that your online presence attracts and retains the interest of your target audience. Here's how to build one.

1. **Set Measurable Goals**: Outline what you intend to achieve; it could be generating website traffic, increasing brand awareness, or boosting product sales. Make sure your objectives are SMART- Specific, Measurable, Achievable, Relevant, and Time-bound.

2. **Know Your Audience**: Research who your target audience is, discover their preferences, interests, and the social media platforms they frequent the most. This knowledge will enable you to tailor your content strategy to align with your audience's taste.

3. **Plan Your Content**: Once you've set your goals and know your audience, the next step is to create a mix of various content types that resonate with your audience.

4. **Analyse Competitors**: Determine what your competitors are doing, especially those who are successfully leveraging social media. Learn from their successful campaigns and avoid the pitfalls they've fallen into.

5. **Schedule Your Posts**: Consistency is key in maintaining audience engagement. Use social media tools to schedule your posts effectively across various platforms.

6. **Engage with Your Audience**: Social media is all about interaction. Respond to comments, ask for feedback, and demonstrate that there's a human behind the screen.

4.3. Creating Engaging Content

Engaging content is an essential ingredient of a magnetic social media presence. But how can you ensure your content sparks interests, prompts responses, and generates shares?

1. **Use High-Quality Visuals**: People are by default visual creatures. Beautiful and eye-catching imagery is a simple but incredibly powerful way to draw people's interest. Don't skimp on quality; now's the time to invest in professional photography or learn how to take great shots yourself.

2. **Write Compelling Captions**: Images may pull people in, but a great caption will keep them engaged. Think about your brand's voice and how you can use it to write captions that intrigue, inspire, or amuse your audience.

3. **Incorporate Video Content**: Videos are an engaging way to convey more information succinctly. Studies show that they keep users on a page for longer and are more likely to be shared.

4. **Use Hashtags Wisely**: Hashtags are key to increasing the visibility of your posts. But remember, quality over quantity is crucial when it comes to hashtags.

5. **Share User-Generated Content**: Sharing content created by your users, such as reviews, photos of them using your product, or testimonials, can significantly boost credibility and authenticity.

4.4. Nurturing Your Online Community

Having an engaged and active online community is the heart and soul of a magnetic social media presence. Here are ways to nurture one:

1. **Encourage Interaction**: Regularly ask your followers questions,

seek their opinions, or create polls to generate interactions. Respond genuinely to their comments and queries.

2. **Share Value-Adding Content**: Posting just promotional content all the time can make your followers lose interest. Try to share informative, educational, or entertaining content that provides value to your audience.

3. **Reward Engagement**: Running contests or giveaways encourages users to engage with your content while enticing potential new followers.

4. **Be Authentic**: Maintain an authentic, consistent voice across all social media platforms. This helps to build trust and loyalty in your brand.

5. **Practice Social Listening**: More than just posting content, social media is about engagement. Listen to what people are saying about you, your industry, your competitors. Respond, align your strategy, or develop new product features based on these conversations.

In conclusion, building a magnetic social media presence requires understanding different social media platforms, crafting a robust strategy, creating engaging content, and nurturing your online community. All of this takes time and effort, but it's worth it for the engagement, branding, and sales potential that can come as a result. Whether you're just starting or looking to refine your existing strategy, you're now equipped with the knowledge to excel at it. Let's get started!

Chapter 5. Viral Content Creation: Step-by-Step Guide

The onset of the digital age has led to an interesting phenomenon - viral content. One could have the most meticulously crafted products or services, but if they're not reaching the online masses, it's like winking in the dark. In this incredibly detailed chapter, you'll be privy to a thorough guide on viral content creation. We'll unravel the process behind generating viral content on social platforms to give your brand a global impact.

5.1. UNDERSTANDING VIRAL CONTENT

To create viral content, it is essential to understand what it is. Viral content is any piece of information, such as a video, image, or post, that rapidly spreads across the internet by sharing and social media engagement. It's characterized by a quick, wide reach and an enormous amount of shares and likes in a relatively short time.

This doesn't happen by accident. Viral content typically has specific attributes that contribute to its rapid dissemination across the wild world of the web. These factors include:

1. Engagement: It triggers an emotional response that incites users to comment, like, and share.

2. Relevance: Viral content often revolves around topics that are current or universally relatable.

3. Shareability: The ease with which content can be shared plays a significant role in its virality.

5.2. THE VIRAL CONTENT CREATION PROCESS

Creating viral content is more than just coming up with inventive posts; it's a structured process that, if undertaken efficiently, can accelerate your brand into stardom.

5.2.1. Step 1: Identify Your Audience

The first step to creating content that goes viral is knowing your audience. Understand their interests, what evokes their emotions, and what they are likely to share. Conduct thorough market research, use social listening tools, and analyse your existing follower base. Once you know what resonates with your audience, you can create content that speaks to them.

5.2.2. Step 2: Choose the Right Format

The next step is choosing the correct format for engagement. Different formats work best for different types of content, and what goes viral on one platform may not on another. For instance, memes travel fast on Twitter, emotional videos trend on Facebook, while stylized photos might generate buzz on Instagram. Consider what formats would be best suited for your content based on your audience and the platform you're employing.

5.2.3. Step 3: Stay Relevant

Keeping up-to-date with trends is an essential step in viral content creation. This doesn't mean blindly following every trend but rather delivering your brand's message through what's current and relatable. Utilize trend-monitoring tools, keep an eye on hashtags, and learn from successful viral content creators for inspiration.

5.2.4. Step 4: Create Engaging Content

Entertainment, inspiration, or information – everything that goes viral offers one or the other. Craft your content to trigger emotion, initiate discussions, use storytelling, or provide valuable information. Make the content interactive and ensure it's easy to share.

5.2.5. Step 5: Timing is Key

The timing of your posts can significantly impact their virality. Publishing content when your audience is most active increases its visibility and hence, the chance of it going viral. Understand the best times to post on each platform and schedule your posts accordingly.

5.3. PROMOTING YOUR VIRAL CONTENT

Once you have created an engaging piece of content that is relevant and shareable, the next crucial stage is promoting it. Here are some methods:

5.3.1. Leverage Influencers

Having influencers share your content increases its visibility, driving more engagement. Influencers' followers trust their recommendations, increasing the likelihood of your content being shared.

5.3.2. Use Paid Advertising

Paid social media promotions can significantly increase your content's reach. Many social media platforms offer promotional services where you can target specific demographics to accelerate your content's virality.

5.3.3. Employee Advocacy

Another strategy to increase the visibility of your content is advocating through your employees. People are more likely to trust content shared by individuals than brands.

5.4. MONITOR AND LEARN

Remember, creating viral content isn't an exact science. Monitor the performance of your posts, learn from your successes and failures, and continually refine your strategy. Virality is not just about one viral post, it's about consistently producing content that resonates with your audience and reflects your brand.

To sum up, viral content creation is a dynamic process requiring an in-depth understanding of your audience, choosing an engaging format, staying relevant, crafting emotional and shareable content, mastering timing, promoting your content, and above all, learning and adapting. When done rightly, it can exponentially increase your brand's visibility and influence. Now, it's your turn to leverage these steps and create a splash in the digital world.

In the next section, we'll delve into the world of viral marketing strategies to amplify your content's reach even further.

Chapter 6. Mastering the Art of Social Media Engagement

Engagement: it's a term that social media marketers throw around, but what does it truly mean? In essence, engagement is the interaction between you and your audience via your posts or the platform itself. It's measured through likes, shares, comments, and overall participation in discussions you've initiated. No matter how many followers you have, it's your engagement rate that determines the success of your strategy on social media.

Understanding the concept and mechanics of social media engagement is the key to unlocking vast reservoirs of potential influence and transforming your online presence from ordinary to sensational. Let's embark on a detailed exploration of the facets, tactics, and nuances involved in mastering the art of social media engagement.

6.1. Engagement Metrics: Understanding the Pulse of Your Audience

It all begins with a deep dive into the metrics that measure engagement, as these numbers are the digital pulse of your audience. Likes, shares, and comments tell you more than you think. You'll uncover what resonates, what falls flat, and what triggers your audience to not only consume your content but also share it, champion it and engage in meaningful dialogue around it.

Likes are the elementary form of engagement, the first reaction from an audience member that shows they took a moment to acknowledge your post. This is a basic level of engagement but it is significant because likes are a form of social proof. A high number of likes can establish credibility and attract more followers.

Comments, on the other hand, signify deeper engagement. They represent an investment of time and thought by your audience. Quality comments often lead to stimulating conversations, which can trigger algorithms to boost your post's visibility.

Shares or retweets represent one of the highest forms of engagement. It means your audience feels your content is valuable enough to share with their own followers, thus extending your reach and impact. Track these metrics and analyze them regularly to determine what content is working best for your brand.

6.2. Crafting Engaging Content: The Art of Attracting Attention

In the ocean of content, it's easy to drown. Standing out requires producing content that your audience finds relatable, valuable, or entertaining. This could be a thought-provoking quote, an educational infographic, a motivating video, or just a simple tweet that humanizes your brand.

One fundamental aspect to consider when crafting content is the concept of value. Ensure that every piece of content you produce either educates, informs, entertains, or inspires. Making your audience feel something after consuming your content can drive them to engage.

Optimized captions are another facet of content creation that can boost engagement. Your captions should provoke thought, inspire action, or elicit emotion. Ask questions, share personal stories, or invite your audience to share their own experiences.

6.3. Harnessing the Power of Hashtags

The right hashtags can extend your reach significantly. They act like magnets, pulling in those who might not be familiar with your brand but are interested in the theme of your content. Start by researching popular hashtags related to your industry and target audience. Even minor tweaks in your hashtag strategy can yield significant changes in your engagement rates.

Before applying any hashtag, remember the "less is more" principle. Overstuffing your posts with hashtags can make them appear spammy and may dilute your message. Select your hashtags judiciously, prioritizing relevance and popularity.

6.4. Utilizing User-Generated Content

Inviting your audience to contribute their own content not only gives you an infinite source of authentic and relatable posts, but it also makes the contributors feel valued and part of your brand's community. When you share user-generated content, make sure to give proper credit to the original creator, as this fosters goodwill and trust.

6.5. Exploring Different Media Formats

Diversifying the types of content you share can also increase engagement. If you're stuck with text-based posts, try venturing into video content or live streams. These formats can offer a more immersive and interactive experience and are more likely to be shared.

6.6. Applying Consistent and Regular Posting

Consistency is key in social media engagement. Regular posting shows your audience that you are active, reliable, and invested in providing them value. Use social media tools to schedule your content in advance and make sure to have a varied mix throughout. This will keep your audience constantly engaged.

6.7. Encouraging Community Participation

Encourage your followers to engage with each other. This can be through shared experiences, general discussion topics, or challenges. When your followers interact with each other, it helps to foster a sense of community, which can lead to increased loyalty and engagement.

6.8. Monitoring, Adapting and Evolving

Finally, no strategy is complete without proper monitoring and assessment. Be sure to analyze your engagement metrics often, and don't be afraid to adapt and evolve your strategy as needed. What works today might not work tomorrow, and staying flexible can help ensure your brand remains in the spotlight.

Remember, the world of social media is ever-changing. However, by understanding your audience, producing engaging content, and optimizing your posting strategy, you can master social media engagement and grow a thriving community around your brand.

Chapter 7. Video Content: A Game Changer for Going Viral

The advent of social media has allowed for a dramatic transformation in the way we communicate and share information. One such tool that has rapidly gained popularity is video content. Akin to a game changer, the impact and reach of video content on social media platforms cannot be overstated. The benefits are manifold, from the ability to deliver complex information in an easily understandable format, to the opportunity to engage users on an emotional level, video content is indeed a remarkable tool.

7.1. The Power of Video Content

Video content, when done right, has the potential to significantly augment your visibility, influence, and ultimately the success of your brand on social media platforms. This form of content allows you to share extensive information in an engaging and interactive way. With apt visuals, appealing graphics, and suitably paced flow of information, video content can prove to be highly engaging, thereby augmenting the chances of its virality.

With videos, the audience is more likely to absorb the information being shared, increasing the chances of recall. In fact, studies have indicated that users are more likely to share, like or comment on video content as compared to other forms of content. Given the emotive factor that videos can induce, effectively crafted video content can deeply resonate with the audience, strengthening the emotional connection and establishing a stronger bond with your brand.

7.2. Key Elements for Successful Video Content

Creating successful video content that resonates with your audience requires integrating key elements that drive engagement and encourage shares. Importantly, your video content must be compelling and deliver value to your audience.

1. Storytelling: Crafting a strong narrative is vital. Your video content should draw in the users through a captivating story that aligns with your brand message and creates a lasting impact. Storytelling through videos allows you to depict scenarios or share experiences that can resonate with the user, making your content a part of their conversation.

2. Engagement: Essential to the success of any social media content, engagement in video content is highly dependent on the format and delivery of your message. Encourage engagement by prompting conditions that foster feedback, opinions, social shares, and likes. Embed interactive elements within your videos - quizzes, surveys, or even shoppable links that trigger user interaction.

3. Quality: High-quality videos that are visually appealing and have superior audio grab the viewer's attention. Good-quality graphic design, clear audio, and a well-paced flow of information can make even a simple video standout.

4. Optimization: Ensure your video content is optimized for each social media platform that you are using. Factors such as length, format, and platform-specific elements can have a significant impact on the performance of your video content.

7.3. The Art of Making Viral Video Content

For your video content to go viral, the creation process needs to be carefully strategized and meticulously executed. Here are a few tips to effectively create viral video content:

1. Understand your Audience: Know who you are creating content for. Understanding your audience demographics, their preferences, and their online behavior can help in creating video content that will resonate with them and eventually move them to share it.

2. Hook them Early: The first few seconds of your video are crucial. Use this time to hook your audience with captivating visuals or intriguing questions that make them want to watch further.

3. Incorporate Emotion: Videos that evoke strong emotions - whether positive or negative - have the potential of becoming highly viral. Let your video content tell a story that touches the hearts of your audience and moves them enough to share with their network.

4. Call to Action: What do you want your audience to do after they've watched your video? Make sure to include a clear and compelling call to action that prompts viewers to share, like, or engage with your content in some way.

7.4. Conclusion

Indeed, video content can be a game changer in making your brand go viral on social media. With strategic planning, understanding of your audience, and careful execution of key elements, you can create a video that not only garners attention and engagement but also effectively communicates your brand message. After all, as the saying goes - a minute of video is worth 1.8 million words. So, if you're striving for your brand to go viral, it's time to harness the power of video content. Make that video worth every view!

Remember, the success of viral content is not just about the number of views, likes, or shares, but also about the impact it makes. It's about crafting content that strikes the right chord with your audience and stays with them long after they've clicked away.

Chapter 8. Influence and Collaboration: The Power of Partnership

The internet has become an interconnected landscape where collaboration thrives. Influence is no longer a one-way street. Instead, it has morphed into a web of interconnections, where one person's voice can trigger a ripple effect of thoughts and ideas far beyond their immediate reach. In this ecosystem, partnerships can propel your message to unthinkable heights.

8.1. Mutual Amplification: Understanding its Significance

Mutual amplification is when two or more entities make use of their combined influence to boost each other's brands. They leverage their online influence to amplify each other's messages. The key to this amplification comes from the increased reach, engagement, authenticity, and richness of content created through such collaborations.

Starting with reach, partnerships can expose your content to a broad and diverse audience. They give your message a chance to land in front of eyes it might have never reached in your immediate network. Furthermore, they extend your reach even to those people who are more likely to be interested in your content - the followers of your collaborator who share similar interests.

Engagement spikes up when your association with an influential partner validates your authority in the eyes of the audience. It gives them a reason to engage, increasing likes, shares, comments, and responses to your content. They also add the midas touch of authenticity. A well-chosen partnership will feel genuine and natural to your audience. As a result, it can cement your brand's credibility.

Finally, collaboration allows for richer and more diverse content. Two minds are indeed better than one! The infusion of fresh perspectives and unique ideas can result in some truly captivating content.

8.2. Choosing the Right Partner

Choosing the right partner is crucial for success in collaboration. This partner would be a person or brand whose voice holds weight in your industry or among your target audience. It's not merely about follower count, but about influence.

You'd need to evaluate the prospective partner based on four main factors: their audience relevance, their content quality, their engagement rate, and their brand affinity.

A partner's audience should be ideal for your brand. Look at their followers' demographics and psychographics. Do they align with your target audience?

Next comes content quality. High-quality content gets more shares, likes, and comments. Hence, evaluate if the potential partner consistently produces high-quality content.

Thirdly, look at engagement rate. A large following with no interaction means little. Check how many likes, shares, and comments their posts usually generate.

Lastly, the brand affinity. Your partner should resonate with your brand and values, thereby ensuring authenticity.

After thorough analysis, propose a mutually beneficial arrangement, and you are ready for the next step.

8.3. Crafting a Collaborative Strategy

Once you've chosen a partner, it's essential to align on a collaborative strategy that defines the purpose, content, and means of promotion. The alliance should be mutually beneficial and clear, focusing on sharing a valuable and appealing proposition to both audiences.

Setting objectives should be the first step in the strategy process. The aim could be to drive traffic to a site, enhance brand recognition, improve engagement, or increase follower count.

The next phase is deciding on the content. It can be anything from guest blog posts, to Instagram takeovers, video collaborations, joint live sessions, podcast interviews, or giveaways. The content should be engaging, valuable, and leverage the unique aspects of both parties involved.

Finally, the promotional strategy. The plan should detail which social platforms will be used, when the content will be released, and how both parties will share and interact with the content.

8.4. Nurturing the Partnership

Maintaining the partnership's dynamics is vital for a sustainable relationship. Mutual respect, continual communication, and acknowledgment of each other's contributions underline the longevity and success of the collaboration. Always remember, collaboration is not a one-time event but a journey.

Positive collaboration experiences bring about continuous partnerships and repeated amplifications. Regular check-ins about performance, brainstorming new ideas, and appreciating and giving public credit to the partner can go a long way.

Remember that the viral trend is steeped in dynamism, and to keep riding the wave, constant innovation, reinvention, and persistence with collaborative efforts are critical. Learn from each endeavour and continually optimize your partnerships to make your message resonate and, indeed, go viral.

In conclusion, collaborations in today's digital landscape are a powerful strategy to amplify your influence and make your brand go viral. Harnessing the right partners and executing a well-planned strategy while nurturing the partnership can unlock this potential and elevate your reach, engagement, and, ultimately, your brand's influence. You are not just sharing content; you are sharing influence, co-creating value, and enhancing your digital presence—so keep your minds open, and your networks interconnected. This is the era of collaborative influence!

Chapter 9. Applying Data Analytics for Social Media Success

Are you ready to harness the power of data to transform your social media strategy? With the advent of big data and advanced analytics capabilities, you can now tailor your messaging to better engage with your target audience. You can leverage metrics to strategize, implement, and optimize your content in alignment with the interest patterns of your followers. So, let's dive deep into the intricacies of data analytics for a successful social media journey.

9.1. Understanding Data Analytics in Social Media

Data analytics, in the context of social media, is the process of collecting, processing, and analyzing volumes of data from your social media platforms to inform business decisions. These insights could relate to user activity, content virality, sentiment analyses, customer interactions, and so much more. Leveraging this data effectively can set the tone for your social strategy and guide your brand towards communication that resonates with your audience.

But, how do you unlock these insights? Where do you start? Enter, data analytics tools. Some popular ones include Google Analytics, BuzzSumo, Buffer Analyze, and Sprout Social. Whether it's crafting targeted campaigns, spotting trends, or forecasting future behavior, these tools can tailor their insights to your specific needs and objectives.

9.2. Identifying Your Key Metrics

First things first, identify your Key Performance Indicators (KPIs). These metrics reflect your objectives and help you measure your online performance against your set goals. Whether it's increasing your follower count, getting more shares/likes, or boosting website visits through your social posts, defining these KPIs sets the foundation for your analytics journey.

But, remember, one size does not fit all. The choice of these metrics varies from platform to platform. For instance, on Instagram, key metrics could be engagement rate, follower growth rate, URL click-through rate, etc. On the other, on Twitter, you might focus on retweet rate, impression rate, or interaction rate.

Here's an illustrative list of some key metrics:

- Followers Count: A tally of individuals who follow your account.
- Engagement Rates: Measures likes, comments, and shares in relation to your following.
- Click-Through Rates (CTR): The number of clicks divided by impressions.
- Conversion Rate: The ratio of conversions to total visitors.

Understanding these metrics and how they tie into your brand objectives will lead the way for a much more targeted approach.

9.3. Leveraging Data for Content Optimization

After identifying your metrics, it's time to deepen your understanding of your audience's preferences, behaviors, and patterns. This is where data analytics can make a significant impact, helping you create and optimize content that has the potential to 'go viral.'

Analyze past performance to zero in on what works for your brand. Pay particular attention to posts with the highest engagement - What was their content? What style was used? Which time did they go live? The answers to these questions can provide formidable insight into your audience's preferences.

Moreover, you can also analyze your competitors' content. Evaluate their high performing posts, successful hashtags, and what their audience responds to. Remember, imitation is not the goal here; gaining an understanding of what resonates with your target demographic is.

9.4. Sentiment Analysis: Finding your Audience's Voice

Sentiment analysis, or social listening, involves monitoring social platforms to understand the public's feelings towards your brand, services, or specific campaigns in real time. Using tools like Brandwatch or Mention, you can gauge emotions, opinions, and attitudes, letting you fine-tune your social media strategy.

Imagine launching a new product. Through sentiment analysis, you can track public opinion, respond to criticism, or express gratitude for positive feedback. It's all about creating a dialogue and making your audience feel heard and connected with your brand.

9.5. Predictive Analytics: Foreseeing Future Trends

As your brand grows and data keeps pouring in, you might want to start thinking about predictive analytics. As the name suggests, it involves using historical data to predict future outcomes or trends.

For instance, based on your followers' activity patterns, predictive tools might foresee the best times to post on different days.

Furthermore, these tools can predict consumer behavior, such as the likelihood of them sharing your content or making a purchase. By leveraging such insights, you can evolve a proactive rather than a reactive strategy.

In conclusion, embracing data analytics for your social media strategy can give you a significant competitive advantage. It can help personalize your approach, make informed decisions, and optimize your campaigns. Remember, in this digital-driven world, "data is the new oil." So, use this powerful resource wisely, and watch your social media presence evolve like never before.

Chapter 10. Cracking the Code: SEO for Social Media

SEO, or Search Engine Optimization, is traditionally associated with enhancing your website's visibility in search engine results. But it's also a powerful tool for boosting your reach on social media platforms, used properly. Understanding the basics of SEO can help you create more engaging, discoverable content, and boost your online influence.

10.1. The Intersection of SEO and Social Media

Consider social media and search engines as interconnected systems that complement each other. Search engines are no longer confined to websites; they permeate social media too. When users search for keywords on social platforms, whether it's Twitter or LinkedIn, the algorithm applies the same mechanics as search engines do.

Social media SEO is distinct, but practices such as keyword optimization, engagement metrics, and high-quality content creation are just as relevant. The objective is to enhance online visibility, capture audiences, and maximize engagement.

10.2. Understanding Social Media SEO

SEO for social media operates on the same fundamentals as traditional SEO: keywords, quality content, and links. But it also offers specific strategies tailored for the unique dynamics of social media platforms.

1. **Keywords:** Like search engines, social media platforms use keywords to help users find content. Using keywords strategically in your posts, profiles, and hashtags can make your content more discoverable.

2. **Quality Content:** On social media, quality content generates shares, likes, and comments. These user interactions can increase the reach and visibility of your posts.

3. **Links:** Links shared on social media can bring traffic back to your website. This can boost your site's authority and improve your search engine rankings.

10.3. Using Keywords for Social Media SEO

Keywords form the backbone of SEO on any platform. They're the phrases and terms that your audience uses to search for content.

To find these keywords, you need to think about what your target audience is likely to search for. This could include industry terms, questions they might ask, or topics they're interested in.

Once you have identified these keywords, include them in your social media posts, hashtags, and profile information. This can make your content more discoverable and attract more followers.

Remember to use keywords naturally. Stuffing your posts with keywords can look spammy and could deter your followers.

10.4. Crafting High-Quality Content

High-quality content is essential for social media SEO. It's the type of content that your audience finds valuable, engaging, and worth sharing.

Creating such content means understanding your audience's needs and interests, and delivering content that answers their questions, solves their problems, or entertains them.

Ways to create high-quality content include:

- Sharing informative articles or blog posts
- Posting engaging photos or videos
- Sharing industry news or updates
- Providing answers to common questions
- Starting a conversation or debate

Each post should have a purpose and meet a need. This could be as simple as spreading joy with a funny meme, or as complex as explaining a difficult concept with an in-depth article.

10.5. Linking Strategy for Social Media SEO

Links are an important part of social media SEO. They can bring traffic back to your website, increasing its authority and subsequently improving search engine rankings.

When you share a link to your website on social media, anyone who clicks that link is directed back to your site. This link is counted as a backlink, which is beneficial for your site's SEO.

Also, encourage your followers to share your links. The more people who share your link, the more visibility your website gets, further solidifying your online presence.

10.6. Measuring Your Social Media SEO Success

Just like traditional SEO, social media SEO requires regular monitoring and adjustment. Use the available tools on your social media platforms to measure how well your SEO efforts are working.

Monitor likes, shares, comments, followers, and website click-throughs to understand what content works and what doesn't. Then, update your strategy accordingly.

Remember, social media SEO isn't about achieving overnight success. It's a long game, requiring patience, learning from mistakes, and recalibrating efforts based on analysis.

10.7. Conclusion

To recap, leveraging SEO strategies for social media involves understanding the symbiosis between both, using keywords wisely, generating engaging content, smart linking, and continually tracking and adapting your tactics. With the right strategies, SEO for social media can massively amplify your digital influence and help your content go viral. The key is to keep learning, experimenting, and optimizing based on your audience's preferences and behaviors.

Keep testing, keep tweaking, and keep growing your digital influence one post, one follower, and one like at a time!

Chapter 11. Risk Management and Ethics in Viral Marketing

The explosive force of viral marketing is a potent tool, but it's not without its risks and ethical quandaries. Managing these effectively can steer your brand clear of negative publicity, legal implications or damage to your reputation. Even better, a sound approach to risk management can boost your chances of success.

11.1. Understanding the Risks

Risk, in its most basic form, stems from uncertainty. In the realm of viral marketing, it pertains to the unpredictable nature of social media and internet users reaction. These risks could range from a failed campaign that leads to wasted resources, to a misunderstood message that generates a backlash.

Most common risks related to viral marketing include:

- Miscommunication or misconception: Your content might end up being interpreted differently than intended. This miscommunication could generate a misunderstandings or negative backlash.

- Damage to brand reputation: Negative perception can severely damage your brand image and trustworthiness in the eyes of consumers.

- Legal complications: Unintentionally infringing on copyrights, privacy rights, or other laws can lead to severe legal repercussions.

Risks | Potential Consequences Miscommunication or Misconception | Misunderstood messages, Backlash Damage to Brand Reputation | Loss of trust, Declined sales Legal complications | Lawsuits, Financial penalties

11.2. Risk Mitigation

Addressing risks in viral marketing involves proactive and reactive strategies. Proactive efforts are preventive and should be undertaken before you launch your campaign. Reactive measures help deal with any fallout effectively.

- Quality control: Rigorous quality checks ensure that your content aligns with your brand values, target audience, and media channels.

- Testing: Run restricted trials or focus group studies to predict the possible public reaction.

- Stakeholder approval: Involving everyone who has a stake in the campaign can ensure a group consensus and reduce individual biases or blind spots.

- Legal Permissions: Acquire necessary licensing to use copyrighted materials, follow privacy laws, and ensure your campaign is legal.

- Crisis management: Develop a contingency plan to manage backlash, misinterpretations, or other threats.

11.3. Navigating the Ethical Landscape

Responsible viral marketing goes beyond complying with laws—it means behaving ethically. While there are no universal ethics that apply to every business and culture, the following broad principles provide a basic framework:

- Honesty: Clear, truthful, and straightforward communication.

- Respect: Show regard for your audience's emotions, cultures, and values.

- Fairness: Avoid manipulations or exploitative tactics.

- Accountability: Admit mistakes openly and rectify them genuinely.

Ethics | Descriptions Honesty | Clear, truthful, and straightforward communication. Respect | Show regard for your audience's emotions, cultures, and values. Fairness | Avoid manipulations or exploitative tactics. Accountability | Admit mistakes openly and rectify them genuinely.

Earning trust from your audience is crucial for successful viral marketing. Building a reputation for ethical marketing can not only insulate your brand from many risks but also significantly enhance its appeal.

11.4. Case Studies

Let's look at a few key case studies that illustrate different aspects of risk and ethics in viral marketing.

1. Dove's 'Real Beauty Sketches': A well-received campaign that promoted a positive body image for women but was later criticized for inadvertently promoting traditional beauty ideals, revealing the risk of miscommunication.

2. Facebook and Cambridge Analytica: An infamous case of unethical data manipulation for viral political content that had massive legal repercussions.

Case StudIes | Risk or Ethical Issue Dove's 'Real Beauty Sketches' | Miscommunication Facebook and Cambridge Analytica | Unethical data manipulation

By considering these challenges presented in Risk Management and

Ethics, brands and marketers can approach viral marketing in a robust and thoughtful way, fortifying their campaigns and brand reputation against potential downfall and ensuring not just viral success, but lasting brand impact.